25 Factors Affecting Business Valuation

By Eric Jordan (CPPA)

Copyright 2017 Eric Jordan

Contents

Acknowledgments

I want to dedicate this book to the teachers and mentors in my life who made me who I am. I am grateful for my mother and father, Fred and Edith Jordan who taught by example. I would like to thank Roy and Earle Hamilton; John Koelle; Reid Nunn; Debby Schlutter; Bill Massey, my cousin; Ange, my daughter; and all the family members who helped me along the way. A special tribute to Charlie Salfries who was my first real mentor and who made me realize I could be whoever I wanted to be. Thanks Charlie.

Preface

This book offers 3 things:

1. **Intangible Assets and Intellectual Property.**
   This book will prove to you that the average business today consists of 70% to 80% Intangible Assets.

2. **25 Factors Affecting Value -**
   I will show you the 25 main factors affecting business valuation that must be measured in order to evaluate a business. Most of these factors are intangibles. I will explain how and why these factors affect the value of a company.

3. **Operations Manual Template - INCLUDED FREE -** Processes, procedures, Systems, and the documentation of those factors are generally contained in what is commonly called an Operations Manual. Having an up to date functional operations manual could add up to 25% more value to your company. It is imperative that everyone have one of these. I have enclosed a free template. This template will help you build your own company specific operations manual that, when filled out, will be the best insurance you could have for your business, your employees, your clients and your family. It will also add thousands, or tens of thousands, to your value. Some larger businesses could gain hundreds of thousands.

Links from real and accredited people and reputable sources, easily verified on the internet, will be provided throughout the book to prove my points with logic and irrefutable evidence. In the e-versions of this book, you can just click the links.

The reader's time will be respected. There should be no empty words, just useful information that is actionable.

Introduction

Procter and Gamble paid 60 million dollars for "The Art of Barber" a small chain of 36 barber shops in 2009. Imagine a barber shop being worth 1.66 million. I did a valuation within this same industry using the 25 factors affecting business valuation. My conclusions were validated when I came across the Procter and Gamble information. This made my client feel very confident in my report.

http://adage.com/article/news/cpg-marketing-p-g-buys-art-shaving-retail-stores/137065/

Price confirmation for the "Art of Barber" sale:

http://wwd.com/beauty-industry-news/beauty-features/gallery/procter-gamble-acquisition-timeline/

Intangible Assets and Intellectual Property are the elephants in the room when it comes to small business valuation. Few valuators are willing to come out of the old-fashioned comfort zone provided by their associations to address the measurement of Intangible Assets. This book will do many things but bear in mind:

I cannot teach wisdom.

I cannot teach experience.

Section 1:

—◆═◇═◆—

Intangible Assets and Intellectual Property:
Intangible Assets make up the majority of the value in most businesses. My objective in this section is to help you understand and accept that it is true. Seventy to eighty percent of the value of your business is intangibles. If this is not true you might want to be concerned.

Intangibles rule the way we live:

Google maps gets you where you are going.
Amazon is the largest store in the world and the owner is now purported to be the world's richest man.
ebay. Who has not used ebay?
Facebook and **Twitter** are two of the most popular and commonly used social networking apps.
AirBnB, **Uber,** and **GrabTaxi** are all "disruptor" business models that changed how things are done.
Netflix has changed the way most people watch television and movies.
Smartphones are streaming data to the masses, including business people.

Intangibles in business
I want to refer you to an internet site that you may not be familiar with unless like me, you have reason to follow such information. Crunchbase.com - Crunchbase reports on funding, mergers, and sales on a more global scale than most information sources ON A

DAILY BASIS, tracking hundreds of millions of dollars in business. Most of these hundreds of millions of dollars that trade daily are intangible assets. Prove it to yourself and look at the website. The following is an example of a daily report.

www.Crunchbase.com - **Daily Newsletter - July 21, 2017**

Klarna raises $225M for payments. Private equity firm Permira will pay $225 million for a stake of at least 10 percent in Klarna, the Stockholm-based online payments unicorn (**Unicorn Pay** is an **online Payment** Gateway Services Provider). Permira will buy shares from existing shareholders General Atlantic, DST and co-founder Niklas Adalberth.

Insurance is a hot space for Venture Capitalists
Funding for insurance-focused startups has shot up dramatically in recent quarters, with a big chunk of investment coming from major insurers, a Crunchbase News analysis finds.

In other news, we look at the massive growth spurt that preceded the latest Series A for loan startup **"Self-Lender."**

Shyp curtails service, cuts staff. On-demand shipping service Shyp announced in a blog post that it is withdrawing from all but one market, the San Francisco Bay Area, and cutting staff at headquarters in what it described as an effort to prove its business model for long-term success. Up till now, Shyp had also been operating in Los Angeles, Chicago and New York.

Betterment closes on $70M. Online financial adviser Betterment has raised $70 million in a new Series E funding led by Kinnevik. The New York-based company has raised a total of $275 million to date.

Recent Activity on Crunchbase
181 Funding Rounds Added
130 Acquisitions Recorded
$2.5B Fundings Captured
12,087 Entities Updated

Make a list of the non-tangible things in your business. It will surprise, if not shock you.
http://www.kmworld.com/Articles/Column/The-Future-of-the-Future/The-world-of-intangible-asset-valuation-110580.aspx

Another link - same conclusion.
https://www.strategy-business.com/article/08302?gko=47f49
60% to 80% back in 2008.

- Employees and client lists are not tangible assets but try to run a business without one or the other.
- What value does a business with a storefront have without a good renewable lease?
- You might have a partner. Without a solid, up-to-date shareholder agreement in place how secure is your investment?
- Did you know that some franchises are for a specific time period of perhaps twenty years? After that you may have only the salvage value of used equipment and leasehold improvements. Your old location might be given to a new franchisee or the franchisor may tell you that in order to continue, you need to move five blocks away into a new building and completely rebuild the store in order to have a new twenty-year franchise agreement. What do you think this sort of franchise is worth in the last four or five years of the lease?

- What is a long-term lease in an airport worth to a high profit food franchise? Add to this some exclusivity and see how that affects things.

- What about Research and Development? The R&D you keep investing in might be written off in the year it was done, but is it gone? Investors in Google and Amazon say NO. Many learned people share the same opinion I do; I hope to prove my points by showing you the profiles of accredited people who have written articles that I believe strongly support and prove my position.

- If you don't have a detailed, well written and up to date operations manual you are probably missing 25 percent of the value of your business. Without a detailed map of what to do, your business cannot run for any length of time without you. Who would want to buy a business without a good operations manual? Who would want to lend money to a company without an operations manual that would allow the company to survive even if the founder was gone? This is one of the reasons why financial institutions prefer financing franchises over independent business startups.

I believe I have proven the point that seventy to eighty percent of the value of businesses today is intangible.

Section 2

These are the 25 main factors affecting business valuation that must be measured in order to evaluate a business. Most of these factors are intangibles. I will explain how and why these factors affect the value of a company. My focus is companies valued at under 10 million dollars.

Factor 1: History
Factor 2: Purpose
Factor 3: Financials
Factor 4: Shareholder Agreement
Factor 5: Value of Employees
Factor 6: Client Base and cost to rebuild
Factor 7: Value of Supply Chain
Factor 8: Value of Distribution Network
Factor 9: Social Network
Factor 10: Dominance in the Marketplace
Factor 11: Processes and Procedures
Factor 12: Company Documentation
Factor 13: Industry Averages
Factor 14: Lease Terms
Factor 15: Leasehold Improvements
Factor 16: Equipment
Factor 17: Inventory
Factor 18: Business Risk including Liquidity
Factor 19: Currency fluctuations and geopolitical considerations
Factor 20: Opportunity
Factor 21: Leverage - Terms and Cost of money.

Factor 22: Minority Interest
Factor 23: Interested Purchaser
Factor 24: Redundancy Management
Factor 25: Return on Investment

Factor 1:
History

⊶❀⊷

T he value of a business starts with the unwritten knowledge of the business founders when they started the business. By digging into their past, we get a glimpse of what unique knowledge they had and what they were attempting to develop. What special talents did the founders have. This can be a big help as we go through the rest of the factors; as we can understand the "purpose" the founders had in mind when they started. In many cases, one will find that there was an unfilled need and a plan to fill the need. History gives us a solid starting point.

Here is a real-world example of history to the rescue:

Kraft Cadbury - history to the rescue.
When Kraft took over Cadbury in 2010 it was not looking pleasant as many Cadbury people were thinking Kraft would dilute the quality. Kraft management went back into the founder's history and showed where the two founders were very similar. They were able to pacify the Cadbury people with the similar beginnings information and it was one of the smoothest mergers Kraft ever undertook. (Read the whole story)
https://hbr.org/2012/12/your-companys-history-as-a-leadership-tool

Factor 2:
Purpose

We need to know the purpose of the valuation to determine what factors are relevant. If the purpose of the valuation is to determine value for the firm and establish a share price to facilitate a new partner coming in; it is different than establishing a price for the purpose of a divorce proceeding.

The divorce proceeding requires we establish a "fair market value" on the legally defined "Effective Date of Valuation." "Terms and Cost of Money" would not be a relevant factor in a valuation for divorce as it is always a cash price used.

A valuation for the purpose of establishing value of shares for a partner coming in, would certainly look at "Terms and Cost of Money" as a relevant factor affecting value. If the "buy in" is 100% financed by the existing partner or partners and the "risk" minimized for the buyer, a higher valuation is likely because of lack of risk.

If I am hired by a prospective buyer of a restaurant; the purpose of the valuation changes. I would look at the value of the business to the current owner, but additionally I would be looking at how the subject business would fit on the new proposed purchaser. In this way, the prospective buyer can make an informed decision about making an offer to purchase. When we look at purpose, this system requires that we ask the question, "value to whom?"

There are no links for this factor as different factors come into play depending upon the purpose or intended use of the valuation.

Factor 3:
Financials

—◄═══❧❦══►—

W hen analyzing financial statements one must adjust the statements to reflect only purchases and expenses at prevailing fair market price that are related directly to the business.

We want to find out if the operation of the business is making money or losing money. We need to know if there are redundant assets that need to be stripped out of the balance sheet. For the purpose of a business valuation we want to look at the balance sheet and income statements. (income statements are sometimes called profit and loss statements)

We will need to normalize the information. Any underpayments, perks or advantages to anyone including owners, friends, and family must be accounted for at fair market. Once everything is adjusted to "fair market" we have what would be called "Normalized Net Income."

Depending upon the situation and purpose we may want to look at 2 to 10 years of financial statements. If auditing is required I suggest an outside accounting firm for that process. The delicate part for small business valuation is "discretionary income."

What to count, how to measure, and what is the purpose.

Determining the "Normalized Net Income" is a real skill set and the first and most important step in determining the value of your small business; any other term implying the same thing is suspect. (Small business being less than ten million dollars in sales.)

If you are reading financial information about a small company and you see the terms, **owner's discretionary income, seller's discretionary income, seller's discretionary earnings, free cash flow, seller's discretionary cash flow or owner's cash flow,** BE CAUTIOUS! These are terms that people feel they can trust but in fact they are often very misleading. You may also see the term EBITDA (Earnings Before Interest, Taxes, Depreciation and Amortization,) this is a legitimate term when used in the right context.

If these terms are used in relation to the sale of a small business, someone (usually the buyer) can be easily misled. The managers of banks and other financial institutions have been misled by these terms so often that their head offices are often very skeptical about financing the purchase of any small business.

OWNER'S DISCRETIONARY INCOME. This term will often be used for those trying to sell a franchise. They will show you a number like $75,000 per year; or perhaps even $90,000 for owning and operating something like a plumbing franchise. What they do not make clear is that the $90,000 per year is BEFORE the owner/manager/PLUMBER is paid. Depending on where you live a plumber will probably make $65,000 to $85,000 a year just by going to work every day.

If the people selling the franchise were being truthful they would use the term "Normalized Net Income" that would show the profit after everything, including the owner's wages, were paid out at fair market value. If the fair market value of the plumber's/owner's wages were $70,000 the true profit figure would be $20,000 not $90,000. The perpetrators are generally white shirt and tie and go to great lengths to convince buyers they are professionals, and in a dark way, that is true.

"Free Cash Flow, Owner's Cash Flow and Owner's Discretionary Income" are all 'weasel' words used in the process of separating buyers from their hard-earned money.

EBITDA (Earnings Before Interest, Taxes, Depreciation and Amortization)

Some industry groups think it is okay to include one owner/manager wage in EBITDA, which results in the same misleading situation. You therefore must be very careful in the context that EBITDA is used, most especially if dealing with small business and the numbers are being explained by a deceitful sales person or owner.

EBITDA is generally used as a measure of a company's operating cash flow based on stated earning from financial statements BEFORE interest, taxes, depreciation and amortization.

https://www.entrepreneur.com/encyclopedia/owners-salary

Here are some searches you may want to do to confirm the conclusions above.

- normalization of financials in a business valuation
- net income after normalization
- owner's income included as company earnings.

Factor 4:
Research & Development (R&D)

Y our R&D was written off on your taxes. Is the R&D really gone? Generally, NOT.

Research and Development in most western nations is written off for tax purposes in the income statement/profit and loss. For tax purposes this is reasonable and lawful.

For the purpose of valuation this is not so true. The value of the R&D did not disappear in the year it was written off. Most often it is added to an existing base of R&D and will be added to again in the next year. It is my opinion that useful lifespan of R&D is somewhere between 5 and 12 years and for the purpose of valuation must be accounted for in the balance sheet as an intangible asset. This means that depending upon the individual business, the valuator will need to make a judgement regarding lifespan of the R&D and adjust the balance sheet to correspond.

I am not the only one to come to this conclusion. Millions of shareholders of public companies and investors in private companies believe this to be true. This is why companies like Uber and AirBnB have such high valuations. People are investing, not because these companies are making a lot of profit, but because the investors believe in the R&D. On the public company side, one could look at Amazon. Not a company returning a lot of profit but certainly a company with lots of R&D that people believe in by the billions of dollars. Not sure how many billions of dollars of proof I would be expected to produce but one could compose a very large list of both public and private companies where the share price or valuation is based upon the perceived value of the R&D.

Unless purchased, Brand is the result of R&D and marketing within. When R&D is part and parcel of a brand, the R&D often has an accumulative value. Uber would be worth much more than the accumulative value of their R&D as would most companies who have developed things and are successful. Stability and growing sales are key to the measure.

Certainly, with any kind of software company, the R&D is of immense value but it may not be shown in the balance sheet. There is a reasonably simple way of looking at this. Many small business owners have both an operating company and a holding company with identical ownership. The holding company generally holds the real estate and possibly other hard assets. The operating company runs the business and pays the operating company fair market value rent on the real estate or other hard assets. The key is, it must be done at fair market value.

For purpose of valuation consider that there is a development company and an operating company both having the same ownership. The development company does the R&D and then sells the R&D to the operating company.

Now you have a measured and identifiable cost item with a receipt that can be placed into the balance sheet as an intangible asset and depreciated at the true use rate of probably between 24% and 12%.

There are some tax rules in different jurisdictions for all of this according to the Association of Chartered Certified Accountants in the UK.

http://www.accaglobal.com/gb/en/student/exam-support-resources/fundamentals-exams-study-resources/f7/technical-articles/rd.html

Under IAS 38, International Accounting Standards regarding R&D an intangible asset arising from development can be capitalised if an entity can demonstrate all of the following criteria:

- the technical feasibility of completing the intangible asset (so that it will be available for use or sale),
- intention to complete and use or sell the asset,
- ability to use or sell the asset,
- existence of a market or, if to be used internally, the usefulness of the asset,
- availability of adequate technical, financial, and other resources to complete the asset, and
- the cost of the asset can be measured reliably.

UK has slightly different interpretations. (See link above)

NOTE THAT WE VALUE R&D FOR VALUATION PURPOSES NOT TAX PURPOSES. SOME OF THE ABOVE WOULD BE OF INTEREST TO THOSE WISHING TO RAISE MONEY AND WANTING TO LEGITIMATELY SHOW VALUE IN THE COMPANY.

Some very bright people have done a lot of research on this subject:

Read the background on them first:
http://www.valens-research.com/about/background/

Now, read what they have to say about capitalization on balance sheet:
https://www.valens-research.com/rd-investment-not-expense-capitalizing-rd-impacts-understanding-corporate-profitability/

https://www.theguardian.com/business/2017/apr/15/tesla-electric-cars-sparks-fly-wall-street-valuation

Factor 5:
Shareholder Agreement

S hareholder agreements are the legal basis for dealing with all matters in a business. Without a legally binding shareholder agreement any dispute can become a seriously costly matter. Minority shareholders are probably the most at risk in a situation where there is no legal shareholder agreement. Just ask any minority shareholder who has been involved in a dispute.

There have been situations where minority shareholders thought their 10% interest in a million-dollar company would be worth $100,000 This is not necessarily true.

When, how, and how much you might recover as a minority shareholder could be half, unless there is a strong legal shareholder document to support your claims. Inversely, majority shares have the possibility of being worth more. Potential for protracted legal wrangling could cause a valuator to come with a lower value than would otherwise result if a proper legal shareholder agreement was in place. There are different sorts of "shotgun" clauses that can be included in these shareholder agreements. Payouts can be over a number of years to make it so the company can afford to pay someone out.

A shareholder agreement that was detrimental to the remaining shareholders could result in a much lower value as well. Have a lawyer you trust review any shareholder agreement before you sign.

Google *"shareholder agreements"* to find anything you are in doubt about.

Factor 6:
Value of Employees

———◄═══❦❦═══►———

C runchbase data shows firms working with AI (Artificial Intelligence) are being funded and trading hands at valuation numbers representing ten million dollars per employee (USD)

Crunchbase.com is not an academic journal but they are the world's only relevant source of data on large tech buyouts and funding updated on a daily basis. Tens if not hundreds of millions of dollars in new deals are posted daily. www.crunchbase.com is free to view.

QHR - Canadian Company Kelowna, British Columbia Canada sold in fall of 2016.
QHR sale ($170,000,000 sale with 200 employees) = $850,000 CDN per employee and rather strongly makes the case that skilled employees are worth something.

Established Web Design and Digital Ad Agency For Sale

South Florida, Florida UNDER OFFER (recent 2017)
Asking Price: $1,245,000 (USD)
Furniture / Fixtures included
Sales Revenue: $780,000 (USD)
Cash Flow: $303,000 (USD)
Asking: $155,000 per employee

This is not to say that every company is worth millions per employee but it is important data to reference. The push for high wages in the restaurant industry is causing the restaurant industry to automate. The employees that are valuable are those who are working on the automation and artificial intelligence robots that will replace the restaurant employees.

Most businesses will fall somewhere in between. Doing the research and understanding the proper measurement for each individual business is a critical exercise in any accurate business valuation. There is a lot of room between zero and ten million dollars for employee value. Employees and contract employees are generally both considered when doing business valuation.

Factor 7:
Valuing Distribution and Client Base

D id you ever wonder why products appear on the supermarket shelf at eye level? There is a whole industry built around product placement. Planogram defines the what, where and how much in retail merchandising. Manufacturers, wholesalers and distributors invest a lot in getting proper visibility on the retail level. The end buyer can also be considered as part of the client base. It can take many years to build a client base that will go looking for the product you want to sell. For the purpose of valuation one must be able to measure the retail purchaser, the retailer, the wholesaler and distributor. How much time and money would be spent to replace what has been achieved. This is why companies buy other companies instead building from scratch.

We should point out that not every factor affecting value is relevant in each individual valuation. One must know what factors are important to measure and what factors are irrelevant for each subject business.

Factor 8:
Value of Supply Chain

First, imagine yourself as the owner of a company importing old Russian military rifles, ammunition, and related items into Canada. Your company is a supplier to retailers and also has an online store. Your supply chain is from the Ukraine. This is about as unstable as it can possibly be with the current geopolitical situation and you are unable to get product. This leaves a very big dent in your business and it is not going to be hard to measure the value.

Second: Imagine yourself as the exclusive Canadian importer of several well know Asian food brands. Sales are strong and everyone is happy. The ties are strong and go back 35 years. This will take a lot more work to measure than scenario one.

Most valuations will be somewhere between these two extremes.

Factor 9:
Social Network - Internet Footprint

L ook at your website. How well does it place on Google for relevant searches? How many views does it get? Is it an e-commerce website? What are the details?

Additionally, there are all of the social networking sites. Facebook, Twitter, LinkedIn, Google+, YouTube, Pinterest, Instagram, Flickr, Reddit, Snapchat, WhatsApp, Quora, Vine, StumbleUpon, and Digg are some of the more popular social media sites.

What percentage of your sales are e-commerce on your own website?

Do you sell e-commerce on other platforms such as Amazon or AliExpress?

If you are a service company, what percentage of your business comes from the internet? If you run a retail store, how much of a role does your website and/or social media play in your customer's decision to come to your store?

Even if this is not a relevant factor it may still be worth considering because you, or someone else, can change this to make it better. This is where the measurement comes in.

Factor 10:
Dominance in the Marketplace

━━◀╌§╌▶━━

Mention ketchup and most people will think of Heinz. That is product domination in the marketplace. Mention search engine and most people will think of Google. That is domination of a service in the marketplace.

Most businesses will not be in such a fortunate situation. Some companies will have 25% or perhaps 75% of the market within a certain geographic area. If so this will certainly increase the valuation.

A fishing license or a dairy quota would have some dominance effect.

There have been issues with cities who issue taxi licenses promising in effect dominance for a particular group who have been "interrupted" by a technology called Uber. The hotel industry is similarly concerned with AirBnB and similar services.

A dominance situation that a valuator will commonly come across is an exclusive lease for a service or retail category in a specific geographical area; something like an airport, university, or shopping centre. Profits are almost locked in for such situations so of course the value is higher as long as the lease is long-term. In some cases, the long-term lease might be the most valuable part of the business. Dominance is not always a relevant factor affecting value.

Factor 11:
Processes and Procedures
Agreements, licenses and other intangible assets

U nless it is a franchise, every company has their own proprietary processes and procedures or something that is patented with a long expiry date. A registered brand or other intangible assets must be measured.

For example, a successful retail bakery in an urban centre has their own proprietary processes and procedures that result in a product that retail clients choose to purchase on an ongoing basis. This is a huge consideration for value. The measurement of some of this is often a ratio depending upon market share or penetration and the means to deliver via employee base. Most franchises today are not doing something so unique; but have simply put very tight processes and procedures into what would often be considered a simple service. Think lawn services, hair salons, tanning salons, pet grooming, sewer pipe cleaning, fencing, car cleaning, car maintenance, and computer repair for just a starter list. Keep in mind some franchises have a defined end date and the franchisor may have no obligation to renew a franchise.

Processes and procedures do not stand alone. There must also be documentation which we refer to next. There is a whole section of this book where we show you a template that can be used to document the processes, procedures and systems of a company.

Factor 12:
Company Documentation

Imagine that you have a fully completed operations manual that documents all aspects of your business. All the processes, procedures and systems are documented. It is done so well that your business runs as smoothly when you are away as when you are home.

Imagine that you run the same business that is just as profitable; but where nothing is documented. As long as everyone is healthy all is well. You can't be gone for weeks, perhaps not even for days without the need to be in constant communication.

The first option offers security of income not only for the owner, family and employees but also security of continued service for the clients. The owner could protect his family from his/her untimely death by having life insurance that is readily available for most business owners. Adequate disability insurance for small business owners is generally too costly and usually not even available. The leaves the owner, family, employees, and clients all at a lot of risk. The more of the operations manual you have completed the better you have protected the future for yourself and all of those around you.

Not all of this would be on a computer but rather printed out with spaces for computer passwords, banking information. Where are the spare keys? Important client and supplier information. The list is comprehensive.

All of the information on each employee's job needs to be documented and regularly updated. This is especially important for the founder of a small business to leave a paper trail for the family to follow. This insures the business will continue if something happens to key players.

A buyer will pay a lot more for a well-documented company than one where the owner says; "I will train you." Sure, and what happens if the owner has a heart attack the day after the sale.

Documentation is so important; a template for making your own small business operations manual is included at the end of this book. FREE GIFT

Factor 13:
Industry Averages

Industry averages are not a relevant factor for all business valuations. One must make sure the comparable data is truly comparable. Air conditioning companies in Miami, Florida are not comparable with air conditioning companies in Seattle Washington.

Many valuators use comparable sales as a major consideration but this can be very inaccurate as the sales figures don't tell you if terms were given, how much net profit was recorded for the preceding years or if owner's wages were included in the profit. Costs can vary significantly.

Unless you are talking about franchises, no two businesses are totally comparable; in fact, most are very different. Being careful to measure data that is truly apples to apples is most important.

Industry averages can provide a guideline. It must be understood that industry averages include both winners and losers and are too broad to provide any sort of accurate measurement for a specific business. In some cases, industry averages will be important but in cases where the business is more unique, the industry averages will mean much less.

Factor 14:
Lease Terms

A business with no lease, or a lease ending soon, has limitations on its value. Costs of relocating could include leasehold improvements, reopening, transferring utilities and associated fees, new equipment and fixtures, to name a few. A strong renewable lease is going to enhance the value of a profitable business. However, a strong long-term lease can choke an unprofitable company. If you sign such a long-term lease and if something else happens (your supply or client base evaporates) you are in a lot of trouble and the lease obligations might offset a lot of inventory that is paid for; your company could be rendered almost worthless.

Also, remember that your landlord is not obligated to renew your lease or let you out of a lease you have signed.

Reading the lease carefully is an important factor in business valuation. When you are considering purchasing a business you had better know the terms of the lease you will be taking over and what the conditions of taking over the lease are. You might want to be renegotiating the lease prior to purchase to make sure you have enough time to make the purchase worthwhile. The reputation of the landlord matters a lot.

A long-term lease negotiated in Calgary just prior to the oil crash can have the effect of making the company worthless to a prospective buyer. In other cases, a long-term lease at a locked in rate can be more valuable than anything else in the company. Lease terms need to be measured carefully in a business valuation.

Factor 15:
Leasehold Improvements

L easehold Improvements have three distinct value classifications and are often valued along with equipment.

- Value within an "operating business."
- Value as "equipment in place" even if the business is not operation, but a reasonable new lease can be negotiated.
- Leasehold improvements and equipment may only be worth "liquidation value" if the business is not operating and you can't negotiate or renegotiate a lease. It is important to note that in "liquidation value" it is important to calculate the cost of liquidation which could run from 20% to 45% of the total received.

If you are opening an upscale spa or upscale restaurant you can expect leasehold improvements sometimes called your "buildout" to be between $300,000 to $1,000,000. In a business valuation one must consider the time left before renovations are necessary again. If for some reason the franchise is lost or the lease does not renew, your leasehold improvements may be of little value. In most cases used equipment is worth very little without a lease.

For accurate valuation one must measure by the correct classification.

Factor 16:
Equipment
Tools, vehicles and other hard assets.

E quipment will generally be listed in the balance sheet along with original cost and depreciated value. Fair market value of the equipment is most often neither of these numbers.

Equipment generally has two classifications;

- equipment value within an operating business, and
- liquidation value.

Equipment, in some cases, would be part of the leasehold improvements and could have extra value as "equipment in place" provided a lease could be negotiated.

Equipment may only be worth liquidation value if the business is not operating. If this is the case it is important to calculate the cost of liquidation, which could run from 20% to 45% of the total received. It is important to know what measurement best suits the purpose of the valuation.

Factor 17:
Inventory

Inventory will generally be valued at cost, however there are many mitigating factors. How marketable is the remaining inventory? What would be the cost of selling the inventory at retail, wholesale, and liquidation.

Inventory within an operating business is going to have more value than "inventory that is in place" or value of inventory net of liquidation. Net liquidation might be 40% less than gross liquidation figure to take into account the costs associated with the liquidation of the inventory. Inventory value within an operating business may be very close to wholesale depending upon marketability factors. One must understand what they are measuring and for what purpose to make an accurate estimate of value.

Factor 18:
Business Risk including Liquidity

A sking all of the right questions and measuring each situation is different and challenging.

Are you in an industry that is or is about to be disrupted. An example would be the taxi business disrupted by Uber. Is your business niche heavy into manual labour that will be replaced by robots and artificial intelligence? Are there new innovative processes and procedures being developed that could replace what your company does. Could your industry niche be outsourced to another country? Competition is of course always a concern unless you have market domination through some kind of exclusivity arrangement. If you lost a big contract could a lender call a loan and put you into a liquidity crisis? If a large contract could not or would not pay, could your business find itself in a liquidity crisis? One must also look at liquid investments as compared to investment in small business that is not liquid. This is a huge consideration for most investors. Who wants to wait 2 years or a lifetime trying to get back money that was invested? This is why ratios are so different between "liquid" or easily sold shares in public companies and shares in private businesses.

Factor 19:
Currency Fluctuations and Geopolitical Considerations

—◄■§§■►—

C onsider a Canadian company importing construction materials from China with pricing in US dollars. Worse yet you are in western Canada, perhaps Calgary. You just signed a long-term lease on a much bigger space. The next month OPEC decides to try and take out the North American oil producers and the oil price tanks. The Canadian dollar tanks along with oil. There is a government in place in Ottawa that is not Alberta or oil company friendly. How do you think this would affect the value of your construction material wholesale / retail operation?

When doing business valuation, it is best to be well-read on business and politics both at home and abroad over a number of years. Understanding the right questions to ask what is important to whatever niche business you are dealing with is essential.

Experience and wisdom cannot be taught.

Factor 20:
Opportunity

Now we can go back to research and development, processes, procedures, systems, employees, how well all of this is documented, and how well it all works together. Risk may of course temper some of the opportunity enthusiasm in the final measurement. Do you know the market trends and where your market niche is going and where you are positioned within that market? When we measure the R&D, processes, procedures, systems, documentation, employees, contractors, and how well all of these factors work together we get an idea of the potential for the company.

Let us suggest you are an internet media company helping people to brand and market their products and services. You have a young and talented team that has been building for six years and are now starting to show significant profit after taking the redundancy out of the system.

The story could of course be exactly the opposite; the profit is in the past, older workforce, losing market share and no R&D to support growth.

Asking the relevant questions and finding out what is going on within the company is the task of the valuator. One does not know until they start the measuring process.

Factor 21:
Leverage - Terms and Cost of Money

D epending on the situation, this factor may not be applicable.

The cost of money is not uniform. A large company may have cash on hand that they are receiving almost zero return on. This makes their cost of capital much different than a small business or individual who might have to pay market rates which could be 5% to 25% depending upon each individual situation.

If your father-in-law has excess retirement money and is willing to support you in your new business venture by loaning you $500,000 to $2,000,000 at 3% you have a huge market advantage going in.

Another thing that can happen is a retiring business owner may decide you are a good manager and he will finance the business at a very reasonable interest rate with almost no down payment. The seller trusts the business is good and that you are a good manager. The seller might feel more comfortable with some of his retirement money still left in the successful business he built.

Compare this to the situation where a buyer must find his or her own money for down payment and borrow the rest at market rates that may be inflated to reflect perceived risk.

Factor 22:
Minority Interest

M ost people think that if you own 40% of the shares in a private company valued at a million dollars that the value of the 40% block is $400,000. Not necessarily so. It depends upon your shareholder agreement and your ability to finance any litigation necessary to enforce that shareholder's agreement. There are judges that might consider your minority shares as only being worth half.

Having a solid shareholder agreement and understanding who you are in business with can save you a lot of pain in the future. As a minority shareholder, how are your dividends going to be paid? Who governs that process? It is a lot easier to buy in than get paid out. There are companies that actively seek to purchase minority shareholder positions at a low price with the intent of negotiating better terms from the majority shareholders who may not want to face protracted litigation against an experienced and well financed minority partner group.

Factor 23:
Special Interest Purchaser

A special interest purchaser is a purchaser who already has assets in place that with this purchase can take further advantage of the efficiencies and economies of scale. If there are significant advantages such as elimination of competition, technology advantages, purchasing power advantages, and a reduction in costs by sharing overhead; then the premium paid will be or could be higher. Most especially higher if there is more than one potential purchaser.

A purchaser who has insider knowledge and information that significantly reduces risk in the marketplace in comparison to an arm's length, third-party buyer could definitely be considered a special interest purchaser. In this definition, the working partners in a small business would all be special interest purchasers if there was a purchase agreement between the owner partners as they all understand the risks and relationships at stake. Because nothing really changes so much there should be high client retention and little risk to cash flow and profit.

An arm's length third party must always be concerned about relationships with both the supply chain and client list.

Factor 24:
Redundancy in Management

W hat is the backup plan for management and how well is it documented? This should all be part of an existing operations manual and part of the company documentation. However, because this point is so important it must be covered again on its own. The higher up the food chain in the company the more extensive we want the backup plan for each management person.

What is the plan for everyone in management and how good does the valuator find it to be. Is the operations manual remotely up to date with computer related passwords?

The valuator must measure what is available and compare it to what should be available.

Factor 25:
Return on Investment

decorative divider

Return on investment is the most important factor and must be considered first and last. From our financial review, we should have found the "Normalized Net Income" if everyone and everything was paid at market value.

We have measured the processes, procedures, systems, documentation, and employees. We have looked at all of the other factors affecting value and we have weighed them up, balancing the risk and opportunity factors. Now we make a determination of what is a reasonable return on investment with all of the relevant factors measured and taken into consideration. Some very large companies such as Amazon have a very high stock price without earnings to justify. On the other end of the scale would be service businesses in an industry that is being trashed.

The valuator must understand and measure accordingly.

Section 3

Operations Manual Template

1. Company Structure.
2. Products and Services.
3. Direct Employees, Contract Workers and Outside Contractors.
4. Licenses, Permits, Accreditation and Certification.
5. Business Suppliers.
6. Clients.
7. Office Procedures.
8. Business Procedures.
9. Business Equipment.
10. Office Equipment.
11. Emergency Equipment.

1. Company Structure

What is the legal structure of the company?
- Proprietorship.
- Partnership.
- Incorporation.
- Public.

Ownership:
- Names.
- Percentages
- Shareholder agreement.

- Where is the legal jurisdiction of the company?
- Where are these documents stored?

Is this a franchise? If yes:
- Where is the franchise agreement?
- What does it say about:
  o Length of time.
  o Selling.
  o Renewal rights.

2. Products and Services

Provide an overview of the products and/or services produced by the business.

3. Direct Employees, Contract Workers and Outside Contractors

Who does the work?
Where is the production of goods and/or services done?
What control do you have?

Direct Employees

Name, and other information.
Date of hire.
Salary, bonuses, and dividends.
Any extra perks?
What do they represent in the company?
What roles do they play?
What are their responsibilities?
Who do they answer to?
Which people would be best able to replace them? Often more than just one person.
In their own words, what exactly do they do?
What confidential information does this person have?

Have they signed a confidentiality non-disclosure agreement - If no - why not?

Computer passwords and other such tech information. This needs to be handwritten on a page with the person's name at the top and kept in a safe place "locked" with an additional copy at your Accountant's and/or Lawyer's office. UPDATE REGULARLY.

Contract Workers and Outside Contractors

Name, and other information.

What is their job description? Include all responsibilities.

What are the terms of their contract?

What special knowledge and information about the company, do they have? This includes relationships, proprietary information they maintain, and of course computer passwords and other access codes.

Professional Services

Lawyer.

Accountant and/or Bookkeeper (taxes, payroll, etc.)

Financial Institutions.

Insurance.

Investment Advisors.

Credit Card Processing.

Collections.

Human Resources.

Media Specialists.

Consultants (including Business Valuator.)

IT Computer Hardware and Software Repair.

IT for Internet presence including social media, domain registration and hosting.

Daily, Monthly and Yearly Tasks

Regarding payments and other financial issues.

Full details required.

Details
Never store sensitive information into software programs that could get hacked. Have printed copies that you have control of at your lawyer or accountant's office. An inexpensive computer and backup drive in your safe might be prudent.

Blue Collar Services
Provide complete details.
Security.
Plumber.
Electrician.
Janitorial.
Landscaping.
Delivery.
Other.

4. Licenses to Operate
City business license.
Other geographic licenses.
Association and industry certifications and licensing.

5. Business Suppliers
Full list and documentation.

6. Clients
Full list in order of importance and/or most profitable.

7. Office Procedures
Opening and closing procedures.
Alarm system passwords and/or codes (need to be handwritten and locked somewhere secure.)

8. Business Procedures

Staffing.

Training.

Order processing and sales procedures.

Call comes in; document what happens after that.

Customer service procedures.

Shipping and receiving.

9. Equipment

List each piece.

Where are the keys?

Who knows how to operate it?

Who repairs it?

Any quirks?

Insurance?

Registration?

Permits?

Lease information.

10. Office Equipment

List each piece.

Computers.

Passwords (handwritten and stored in a secure location.)

Maintenance.

Where you purchase the consumables.

Lease information.

11. Emergency Procedures

Full details including muster stations.

In case of fire.

In case of earthquake.

Conclusion

This book should have helped you to understand that it is mostly the intangibles in a business that determine the value. Depending upon the reason or purpose that caused you to read this book, you will determine how you utilize the information. If you are a business owner, this book will have given you some clarity on what is valuable in your own business. Just by understanding this you will know where you should invest your time.

If you put some time into developing an operations manual from the free template in Section 3 you are likely to be gaining tens of thousands of dollars (or more) in value from documenting all these things.

Lawyers, lenders, and accountants will know which clients will benefit the most from reading this book and point them in the right direction.

Divorce litigants and others in dispute will better understand their own situation and be better able to make decisions going forward.

> I cannot teach wisdom.
> I cannot teach experience.

If, however, you are stable, motivated and feel you have enough wisdom and experience to qualify, I am open to training associates anywhere in the world. www.pin.ca

www.ingramcontent.com/pod-product-compliance
Lightning Source LLC
Chambersburg PA
CBHW070947210326
41520CB00021B/7099